Mercury, Mars
and Other
Inner Planets

Chris Oxlade

WAYLAND

First published in Great Britain in 2007
by Wayland, an imprint of Hachette Children's Books

Hachette Children's Books
338 Euston Road, London NW1 3BH

Editor: Nicola Edwards
Designer: Tim Mayer
Consultant: Ian Graham

British Library Cataloguing in Publication Data
Oxlade, Chris
    Mercury, Mars and other inner planets. - (Earth
    and space)
    1. Inner planets - Juvenile literature
    I. Title
    523.4

ISBN-13: 9780750249218

Cover photograph: Mars, the fourth planet from the
Sun, is known as the 'red planet' because its surface
is covered with red-brown rock and dust.

Photo credits: ARC/NASA: 37t. Brooks Kraft/Corbis:
42. John Conrad/Corbis: 26-7b. Corbis: 26t, 30t.
Creasource/Corbis: 38. ESA: 24, 25b, 36. ESA-AOES
Medialab: 17b, 25t. ESA/IASF, Rome , Italy and
Observatoire de Paris, France: 19t. ESA/MPS,
Katlenburg-Lindau, Germany: 7. ESA/STARSEM-
S.Corvaja: 41. Guntmar Fritz/zefa/Corbis: 43. Mark
Garlick/SPL: 11t, 31b. Calvin J. Hamilton/ESA: 15.
David A. Hardy/SPL; 34. Roger Harris/SPL: 21b.
JPL/NASA: 1, 8, 9, 14, 16, 17t, 20, 28t, 33, 35, 37b, 39,
40. Lunar and Planetary Laboratory/NASA: 4. NASA:
5, 12, 13, 19b, 44t, 44-45b.
NASA/GSFC/METI/ERSDAC/JAROS and US/Japan
ASTER Science Team: 23. NASA/JPL/NIMA: 22.
NASA/KSC: 28b. NASA-MSPC: 18. Roger
Ressmeyer/Corbis: 29. Reuters/Corbis: front cover. US
Geological Survey/NASA: 32 US Geological
Survey/SPL: 10.

Every attempt has been made to clear copyright.
Should there be any inadvertent omission please
apply to the publisher for rectification.

The website addresses (URLs) included in this book
were valid at the time of going to press. However,
because of the nature of the Internet, it is possible
that some addresses may have changed, or sites may
have changed or closed down since publication.
While the author and publisher regret any
inconvenience this may cause the readers, no
responsibility for any such changes can be accepted
by either the author or the publisher.

Contents

Rocky Worlds

The Earth is an enormous planet. But it is only enormous on our human scale. In the vastness of space it is a tiny place. It is just one member of a whole family of planets. Together with the Sun, these planets make up our Solar System.

Inner planets and outer planets

There are eight planets in our Solar System. Some are smaller than Earth, and some are far larger. Only two planets, Uranus and Neptune, look similar to each other. All the other planets have their own unique features. However, we can divide the planets into two main groups.

The four inner planets drawn at the same scale as the Sun.

The first group is made up of the four planets nearest the Sun: Mercury, Venus, Earth and Mars. These planets have solid, rocky surfaces. They are known as the inner planets, the rocky planets, or the terrestrial planets. These are the planets we look at in this book.

The second group is made up of the four planets much further from the Sun: Jupiter, Saturn, Uranus and Neptune. These gigantic balls of gas are known as the gas giants.

Pluto, a small, icy body beyond Neptune, was classed as a planet until 2006. Then experts at the International Astronomical Union downgraded it to a 'dwarf planet' as it is just one of thousands of similar objects in the same region.

Rocky surfaces

The inner planets are Mercury, Venus, Earth and Mars. They all have surfaces made of solid rock. Mercury is the smallest rocky planet. Its surface is covered with craters, like our Moon. Venus is smothered by a thick atmosphere. Beneath the atmosphere is a surface covered with lava flows. Mars is covered with red-brown rock and dust, and has giant volcanoes and canyons. Earth is very different to these other rocky worlds. It is the only place with oceans of liquid water, moving tectonic plates, and life.

Moons

A moon is a large rocky body that orbits a planet. Earth has one large moon (known as the Moon), and Mars has two tiny moons, Phobos and Deimos.

The inner planets (from back to front, Mercury, Venus, Earth and Mars).

How do we know?
Rocky surfaces

Apart from the Earth, our neighbours in space, Venus and Mars, are the two planets we know most about. Dozens of robot probes have visited each planet, mapping their surfaces, photographing their surface features, and analysing their rocks and atmospheres.

Moving Through Space

All the planets move around the Sun in paths called orbits. They all orbit in the same direction. The orbits are not exactly circular, but slightly squashed. The planets also spin as they move through space.

Planet orbits

The closer a planet is to the Sun, the faster it moves around its orbit. Mercury travels around its orbit twice as fast as Mars, and completes its orbit in one eighth of the time. The Sun is not at the centre of the squashed orbits of the planets. Instead, it is slightly over to one side. So as a planet orbits the Sun, it moves slightly closer and then slightly further from the Sun. Of all the inner planets, Mercury's orbit is the most squashed.

The orbits of the inner planets (shown as circles).

Spins

The planets also spin as they orbit. Each spins around its axis, which is an imaginary line through the planet. A planet's poles are where its axis comes out through the surface. The Sun lights up the side of a planet nearest to it. As the planets spin, places on their surfaces move in and out of sunlight, giving day and night. The moons also spin as they orbit.

The Earth's spin makes the Sun and stars appear to move across the sky as time passes. You would see the same movement of the Sun and stars from the surfaces of the other planets, but at different speeds.

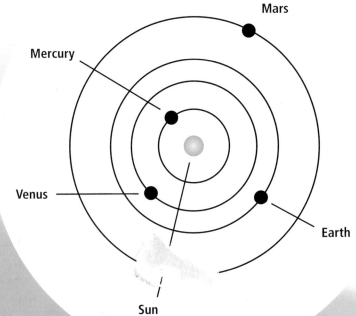

Mars

Mercury

Venus

Earth

Sun

A photograph of the south pole of Venus. It is day on the left side, lit by the Sun, and night on the right side, in shadow.

Days, months and years

The movements of the Earth and Moon give us days, years and months. A day is the time the Earth takes to complete one spin. A year is the time the Earth takes to complete one orbit of the Sun. A lunar month is the time between one New Moon and the next.

Gravity

The force of gravity keeps the Earth and Moon in orbit. Gravity attracts the Earth to the Sun, and the Moon to the Earth. It acts like a string, stopping the Earth and Moon from flying off into space, and making them move in a circle. At the same time, because the Earth and Moon are moving along their orbits, they do not fall towards the Sun or Earth.

SPACE DATA

Inner planet records

Fastest planet: Mercury (48 km per second)

Slowest spin: Venus (243 Earth days)

Fastest spin: Earth (23 hours, 56 minutes)

Longest year: Mars (687 Earth days)

Shortest year: Mercury (88 Earth days)

How the Planets Formed

Astronomers think that all the planets in our Solar System were formed about 4,600 million years ago, soon after the Sun was formed. All the inner planets began life as balls of hot rock.

Birth of the Solar System

Our Solar System formed nearly 5 billion years ago from part of a vast cloud of gas and dust called a nebula. Gravity slowly pulled the gas and dust together into clumps. The clumps also began to spin. Gravity continued to work, pulling the clumps into extremely dense balls of material. Intense heat and pressure in the centre of the balls started nuclear reactions. Energy from the reactions produced heat and light, so the balls began to shine. One of them was our Sun.

Planetesimals

The Solar System formed from a cloud of gas and dust like this, million of kilometres across.

Astronomers think the planets formed from a disc of material left over after the formation of the Sun. This disc was spinning round the Sun, like a spinning CD. It was made of particles of rock, dust and gas. When two particles collided, they sometimes stuck together, forming larger particles. Very slowly, gravity pulled these larger particles together. Eventually large boulders formed. These are known as planetesimals. They were the building blocks of the planets.

Space facts

- Earth probably had as many craters as Mercury in its early life. They have been wiped away by volcanic eruptions and erosion.

- The planets turned out differently to each other because they contained different mixtures of chemicals, were different sizes, and were different distances from the Sun.

Eventually, gravity pulled the planetesimals together to make the planets. Overall it took 100 million years for the planets to form. The material left over from the disc around the Sun also formed the moons around the planets, and all the other bodies in the Solar System, such as the asteroids and comets.

The early planets

The inner planets had surfaces of molten rock when they were formed. The surface rock gradually cooled as heat from the rock escaped into space. Eventually the liquid rock solidified, forming solid rock. This formed a solid crust all over the planet, with hot rocks underneath.

The space between the planets was filled with planetesimals and smaller lumps of rock. These regularly collided with the young planets, raining down on their surfaces, and smashing holes in them. Gradually, over hundreds of millions of years, the bombardment subsided. We can still see hundreds of these craters on Mercury and the Moon.

Rocks on the surface of Mars, formed when molten rock cooled on the planet's surface.

9

Mercury

Mercury is the closest planet to the Sun, and the smallest of the inner planets. It is roasted by the Sun's intense heat. We don't know as much about Mercury as we do about most of the other planets. Only one space probe has ever visited the planet, in the 1970s.

Mercury's orbit

Mercury moves around the Sun in a very squashed orbit. At one side of its orbit, Mercury is 70 million kilometres from the Sun, and at the other side, it is just 46 million kilometres from the Sun. Mercury completes an orbit in just 88 Earth days. It travels through space at an incredible 48 kilometres per second. Mercury spins extremely slowly compared to the Earth. It takes more than 58 Earth days to complete one spin.

Strange effects

Mercury's fast orbit and slow spin cause a very strange effect. On Earth, the Sun rises and sets 365 times a year. But on Mercury the Sun rises one year and sets the next year! The time from one sunrise to the next (called a solar day) is 176 days on Mercury. Because a Mercury year lasts just 88 Earth days, on Mercury, you could have two birthdays every day! After a place on Mercury's surface moves into the sunlight, the slow spin means that it stays in the sunlight for an orbit and a half before the sun sets again. Mercury's squashed orbit also means that the Sun sometimes appears to go backwards across the sky.

A map of one side of Mercury made up from photographs taken by the Mariner 10 *probe in the 1970s.*

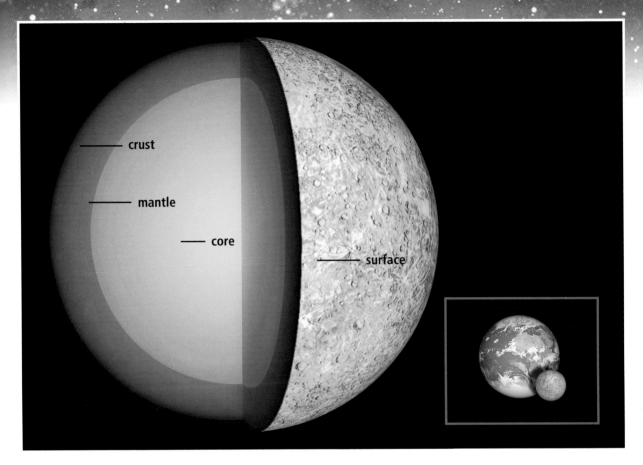

crust

mantle

core

surface

Mercury's structure

We don't actually know what the inside of Mercury looks like, but we can make some assumptions. We can assume that the internal structure is similar to Earth. That means there is a thin outer crust, a thick mantle underneath, and a core in the centre. Astronomers have calculated the mass of Mercury from observing how it affects the orbit of Venus. From that, they think that Mercury has a dense, iron core that makes up 80 per cent of its mass. Mercury has an extremely thin atmosphere. The *Mariner 10* probe and observatories on Earth have detected oxygen, sodium, hydrogen, helium and potassium in the atmosphere, but so far we don't know how much of each.

This is what astronomers think the inside of Mercury looks like.

SPACE DATA

Mercury

Diameter:	4,879 km
Average distance from Sun:	57,910,000 km
Time to complete one orbit:	88 Earth days
Time to complete one spin:	58.6 Earth days
Gravity at surface:	0.38 x Earth gravity
Surface temperature:	-180°C to 430°C
Number of moons:	0

Mercury: the Surface

Only a little more than half of Mercury's surface has been mapped. The part we have seen looks very much like the Earth's Moon.

Mercury has a complex surface made up of plains and ridges, along with thousands of craters.

Mercury's craters

Most of Mercury's craters were formed in its early life. But some of Mercury's craters are much younger. We know this because we can see lines of rock and dust spreading out from the craters. Craters like this are called ray craters. Mercury's craters were made billions of years ago, but they are still visible because there is no flowing water to wear them away, and no volcanoes to erupt and cover them with lava. Mercury's surface also has flat plains, formed when lakes of molten lava cooled in the planet's early history.

The Caloris Basin

The largest feature on the surface of Mercury is a giant impact crater called the Caloris Basin. It is 1,350 kilometres wide. The gigantic impact that created the basin threw up rings of mountains around the crater, up to 2,000 metres high. The impact was so huge that its effects can be seen on the opposite side of Mercury. Shock waves passed right through the planet like a super-powerful earthquake, creating ripples in the surface on the opposite side.

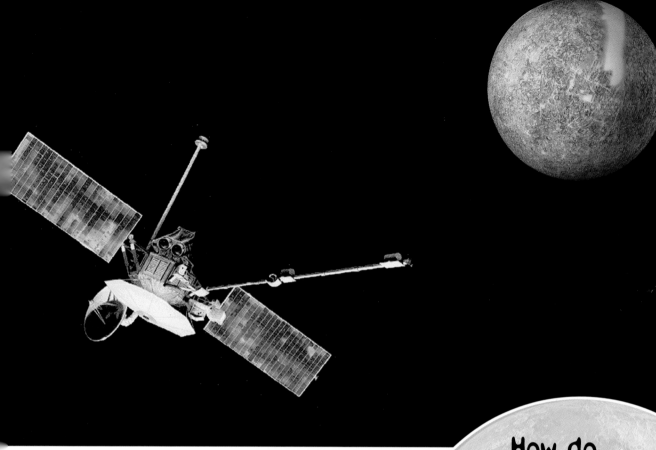

An impression of Mariner 10 *flying past Mercury. The large shade protected the probe from the intense heat of the Sun.*

Mercury cliffs

Mercury's surface also has ridges and lines of cliffs, called scarps. These ridges and scarps are often several kilometres high and hundreds of kilometres long. They were probably formed when Mercury's core cooled and shrank. This made the crust too large for the planet, and it wrinkled up.

Hot and cold

Because Mercury spins so slowly, places on its surface are exposed to the heat of the Sun for a long time. The surface temperature rises to an incredible 430 degrees Celsius. When the same places finally move into the dark, the temperature drops to −180 degrees Celsius. Despite the heat, there may be frozen water in craters near the poles.

How do we know?

Mariner 10

Mercury is the least explored of the inner planets. Only one space probe, *Mariner 10*, has visited, in 1975. *Mariner 10* used the gravity of Venus to get into orbit round the Sun, and it flew by Mercury three times. It took thousands of photographs, but of only one side of the planet. The *Messenger* probe is due to visit Mercury in 2011.

Venus

Venus is the second
planet from the Sun.
It is almost the same
size as the Earth,
and its mass is
almost the same,
too. But Venus is a
very different
world to the Earth.
It has a dry surface,
a thick, choking
atmosphere, and a
surface hotter even
than Mercury's.

Venus's orbit

Venus takes 225 Earth days to
complete one orbit, so its year is
about two-thirds the length of an Earth
year. But the way it spins is very different to the
way the Earth spins. Venus spins extremely slowly. It completes a
spin only once every 243 Earth days. It also spins in the opposite
direction to all the other planets. This is known as a
retrograde spin. It means that the Sun rises
and sets only twice in each year.

*A false-colour image of
the surface of Venus.
The pink areas are the
highlands and the blue
areas are the lowlands.*

Internal structure

Astronomers think that the
internal structure of Venus is
like the internal structure of
the Earth, with a core, mantle
and crust.

SPACE DATA

Venus

Diameter:	12,103 km
Average distance from Sun:	108,200,000 km
Time to complete one orbit:	224.7 Earth days
Time to complete one spin:	243 Earth days
Gravity at surface:	0.9 x Earth gravity
Surface temperature:	464°C
Number of moons:	0

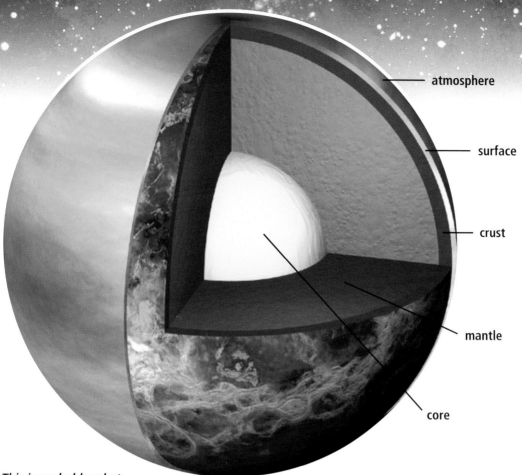

atmosphere

surface

crust

mantle

core

This is probably what the inside of Venus is like. The surface is hidden by the thick atmosphere.

They assume this because it is the almost the size and mass as the Earth, and was formed at the same time. The core is made mostly of iron. Around the core is a mantle of rock. Covering the mantle is a crust. The top part of the mantle is probably molten. This molten rock leaks through the crust in some places, causing volcanoes.

Seeing Venus

Venus is the one of the easiest planets to see. It looks like a very bright star. Because it is closer to the Sun than Earth, it is always close to the Sun in the sky. It can sometimes be seen low in the eastern sky just before the Sun rises, or low in the western sky just after the Sun sets. This is why Venus is known as the morning star or evening star.

The Sun lights only one side of Venus. From Earth we see different amounts of this lit side as Venus moves around its orbit. Sometimes we see nearly a full circle of light, sometimes a semi circle, and sometimes a thin crescent. These shapes are known as phases.

Venus: the Surface

The surface of Venus is quite smooth compared to the surfaces of the other rocky planets. It is dry and strewn with rocks and boulders. It is far too hot for liquid water, which would evaporate instantly. There are very few craters.

Venus volcanoes

Tens of thousands of volcanoes litter the surface of Venus. They may still be active, but because the surface is hidden by cloud, we can't see any eruptions that do happen. Astronomers think that the surface is quite smooth because it has been covered by lava flowing from the volcanoes. This may have happened in the last few hundred million years. The lava has buried most of the craters on the surface. Among the numerous volcanoes are several giant volcanoes which are hundreds of kilometres across.

Volcanic activity has also caused mounds on the surface, where magma under the surface has pushed upwards but not broken through. The mounds, known as pancake domes, are covered with cracks where the surface has stretched. Around the volcanoes are tall, solidified lava falls (like frozen waterfalls).

A three-dimensional image of a volcano on Venus called Maat Mons, mapped by the Magellan *probe using radar.*

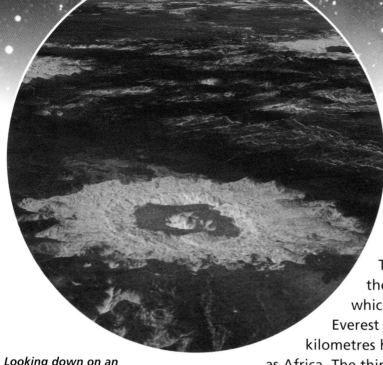

Looking down on an impact crater on the Lavinia Planitia plain on Venus.

Highlands and mountains

Venus has highland regions that stand above the vast flat plains. The two largest regions are called the Ishtar Terra and the Aphrodite Terra. The Ishtar Terra contains Maxwell Montes, the highest mountain on Venus, which is 11 kilometres high (Mount Everest on Earth is just under 9 kilometres high). Aphrodite Terra is as large as Africa. The third highland area, called Beta Regio, contains the two largest volcanoes on Venus, each 4 kilometres high and hundreds of kilometres across. In some places the surface is cracked and rippled, and in others there are deep valleys, probably caused by the surface being pulled apart in the distant past.

Venus in the past

In its early life, the surface of Venus may have looked a little like the Earth today. It may even have had oceans of liquid water. But the Sun's heat would have evaporated the water, and also caused the thick atmosphere to form. This is why Venus turned into such a different planet to Earth.

An impression of the Venus Express probe orbiting Venus.

How do we know?
Magellan and Venus Express

Much of our knowledge about the surface of Venus came from the *Magellan* probe that went into orbit around Venus in 1990. It used radar to measure the distance to the surface as it orbited, and so built up a three-dimensional map of the surface. *Venus Express* arrived in 2006 to investigate how the atmosphere works, and to search for volcanic activity.

Venus: the Atmosphere

Venus is surrounded by a thick atmosphere, full of clouds that block our view of the surface. The atmosphere is very dense, and it works like a greenhouse, trapping heat from the Sun. An astronaut on the surface of Venus would be crushed by the pressure and roasted by the heat.

Gases of the atmosphere

The atmosphere on Venus is very different to Earth's atmosphere. It contains much more gas than Earth's atmosphere. This makes the atmospheric pressure at the surface ninety times the atmospheric pressure on Earth.

This photograph of Venus's swirling clouds was taken by Mariner 10 *as it flew by on the way to Mercury.*

The gases are different, too. Carbon dioxide makes up ninety-six percent of Venus's atmosphere. Most of the rest is nitrogen. There is no oxygen, so astronauts could not breathe on Venus, even if they could survive the pressure and heat.

Sulphur clouds

Fifty kilometres above the surface of Venus there is a thick layer of cloud, 19 kilometres thick. The clouds never part to let us see the surface. They are made up of droplets of sulphuric acid. Acid rain falls from the clouds, but it never reaches the surface because the drops evaporate as they fall.

At the level of the clouds, severe winds blow at more than 350 kilometres per hour. That's more than hurricane force. Even though it takes 243 Earth days for Venus to complete one spin, the clouds whiz round the planet in just four Earth days.

A composite photograph of Venus's southern hemisphere. The right half shows heat coming from the clouds.

The greenhouse effect

On Earth, carbon dioxide and other gases in the atmosphere trap heat from the Sun. This is known as the greenhouse effect. It keeps the atmosphere warm. The greenhouse effect also happens on Venus. But because the atmosphere is so thick, and mostly carbon dioxide, the effect is extreme. It heats the atmosphere at the surface to a blistering 464 degrees Celsius. This makes Venus the hottest planet in the Solar System, even though it is twice as far from the Sun as Mercury.

How do we know?

Venera probes

A series of probes launched by the Soviet Union explored Venus in the 1960s, 1970s and 1980s. The first three failed to reach Venus. *Venera 4* was the first probe to enter the atmosphere and send back data. *Venera 7* was the first probe to land successfully and send back data, although it was destroyed by heat and pressure after 23 minutes. *Venera 9* survived long enough to transmit the first-ever photograph of the surface.

A photograph of the surface of Venus, taken by the Venera 14 probe in 1982.

ВЕНЕРА-14   ОБРАБОТКА ИППИ АН СССР И ЦДКС

Earth

Earth is the third planet from the Sun. It is the largest of the inner planets. Earth's blue oceans and green vegetation make it look very different to the other planets. It is the only place in the Solar System with oceans of liquid water, with a surface that is constantly changing, and, as far as we know, with life.

The Earth from space. The vast oceans give the Earth its nickname, the 'Blue Planet'.

Earth's orbit and spin

The Earth completes one orbit every year, or 365.26 days. The orbit is almost circular. The Earth completes one spin every 23 hours and 56 minutes.

Earth's structure

The Earth is a giant ball of rock, made up of four layers. We stand on the top layer, which is called the crust. Under the Earth's continents, the crust is 35 kilometres thick on average. It is only a few kilometres thick under the oceans. Under the crust is the mantle. This is nearly 3,000 kilometres thick, and it makes up about three-quarters of the mass of the Earth. The rocks in the top layer of the mantle are partly molten because they are so hot. They flow very slowly, which makes the crust above move about. You can find out more about the moving crust on page 22.

Beneath the mantle is the core, which is divided into the inner core and outer core. Together they are about 7,000 kilometres wide. The core is made mostly of iron. The outer core is molten, and the inner core is solid.

The early Earth

When the Earth formed, its surface was molten. Gradually heat escaped into space from the surface. This made the surface cool and solidify, forming a crust. Meteorites smashed holes in the surface, releasing lava from underneath, and keeping the surface hot. It is likely that one massive collision smashed off a piece of Earth, forming the Moon. At the time the Earth was covered with craters, like Mercury is today. There was no atmosphere, no oceans, no mountain ranges, no rivers, and no life. Over billions of years the Earth has transformed into the planet we know today.

SPACE DATA

The Earth

Diameter:	12,756 km
Average distance from Sun:	149,600,000 km
Time to complete one orbit:	365.3 days
Time to complete one spin:	23 hours 56 minutes
Gravity at surface:	9.81 m/s^2
Surface temperature:	-70°C to 55°C
Number of moons:	1

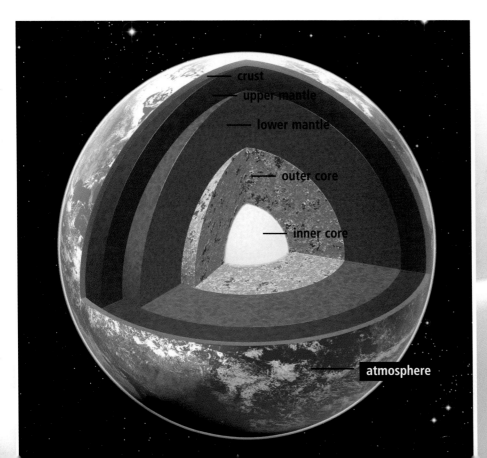

crust
upper mantle
lower mantle
outer core
inner core
atmosphere

We know about the internal layers of the Earth by measuring how shock waves from earthquakes bounce around inside it.

Earth: the Surface

The Earth's surface is very different to the surfaces of the other rocky planets. The main differences are due to water. It fills the oceans, forms ice caps, and cuts river valleys. The Earth's surface is always changing, too. New crust is made, mountains are built up, and the landscape is worn away.

Oceans, rivers and ice

Oceans cover two-thirds of the Earth's surface, and contain 97 per cent of all the Earth's water. The Pacific Ocean covers nearly half the surface on its own. On the land, flowing rivers cut valleys and deep canyons into the surface. They also build up features, such as floodplains and deltas. Ice rivers called glaciers also cut valleys in the mountains, and ice forms sheets thousands of metres thick at the poles.

The San Andreas Fault in California, USA, where two tectonic plates slide slowly past each other.

Tectonic plates

The Earth's surface is the top of its outer layer, the crust. The crust is made up of several giant pieces, called tectonic plates. Movements in the molten rock under the crust make the plates move very slowly. This movement is called continental drift. As far as we know, the Earth is the only planet with tectonic plates. Earthquakes happen when the moving plates become jammed and then move suddenly.

Over hundreds of millions of years the plates have moved thousands of kilometres around the globe. Millions of years ago the continents were all bunched together, before they moved to their positions today.

Building mountains

In some places the edges of two plates move towards each other. The edges of the plates crumple up, forming giant mountain ranges such as the Himalayas and the Andes. Mountains are also built up by volcanoes. These normally happen at the edges of tectonic plates, where molten rock is forced to the surface.

Eroding away

The landscape is worn away by a process called erosion. Rocks are broken up by the heat of the Sun, by freezing water, and by being hit by other rocks blown by the wind or carried by water. The loose rock is carried away by the wind, water or pulled downhill by gravity.

The changing surface

Together, the moving tectonic plates and erosion have created all the features on the land, such as mountain ranges, river basins, valleys and plains. In millions of years' time they will have created a completely new surface that we would not recognise.

Earth Facts

Earth's features

● The Himalayas were pushed up when the Indian tectonic plate collided with the Asian plate. The mountains are still rising by about 6 millimetres per year.

● The Earth's tectonic plates move at a few centimetres a year — about the same speed that your fingernails grow.

A satellite view of mountains of the Tibetan Plateau, which was pushed up as India collided with Asia.

Earth: the Atmosphere

Energetic tropical storms like this form when the air gains heat and water vapour from the warm oceans underneath.

The Earth's atmosphere is a layer of gas that covers the Earth. The atmosphere is vital for life on Earth. It contains gases that plants and animals need to live, it keeps the Earth's surface warm, and it protects life from harmful rays coming from the Sun.

Gases of the atmosphere

Nitrogen makes up 78 per cent of the air, and oxygen makes up 20 per cent. The remainder is made up of many different gases, including carbon dioxide. There is always some water vapour in the atmosphere, too.

The atmosphere is most dense at the Earth's surface. Above the surface the atmosphere becomes thinner and thinner, until it runs out, and space begins, about 100 kilometres up. In the upper atmosphere, there is a special form of oxygen, called ozone, that stops much of the harmful ultraviolet radiation from the Sun from reaching the surface.

Earth Fact

Earth's atmosphere

● An aurora is like a curtain of light in the sky. Auroras are seen near the poles. They happen when particles from the Sun smash into gas in the upper atmosphere, releasing light.

The weather

Winds, clouds and rain all happen in the lowest level of the atmosphere, which is about 10 kilometres thick. The Sun heats some parts of the surface more than others. The surface heats the air above. This makes the air rise and swirl about, causing winds and weather systems. Water from the oceans and the land evaporates into the air, forming water vapour, which is carried along by the wind. When the air cools, the water vapour condenses to form clouds.

The Sun's rays are weak at the poles, and the air never gets warm enough to melt the ice caps.

Climates and seasons

The pattern of weather a place on Earth has is called a climate. Close to the equator, the climate is tropical, with warm, wet weather all year. Close to the poles, the climate is polar, with very cold weather all year. In between, most places have warm summers and cool winters. These seasons happen because Earth's axis is tilted over to one side.

A place has summer when the pole it is nearest to is tilted towards the Sun. On the opposite side of the orbit, this pole is tilted away from the Sun. Then it receives less heat, and it is winter. When it is summer in the northern hemisphere, it is winter in the southern hemisphere, and vice versa. Earth's tilt also means that there are more hours of sunshine in summer than in winter.

A tropical island seen from space. The land is covered with thick vegetation that grows in the warm, rainy climate.

Earth: Water and Life

All animals and plants on Earth are made up of mostly of water. Scientists believe that life can only exist where there is a supply of liquid water. As far as we know, Earth is the only planet or moon in the solar system where there is liquid water, and where there is life.

Earth's water

There is liquid water on Earth because the Earth is just the right distance from the Sun, and because the atmosphere keeps the Earth warm. If the Earth were closer to the Sun, the water would boil away in the heat. If it were further away from the Sun, all the water would be frozen, as it is in the polar ice caps. The region in the Solar System where liquid water can exist on a planet is known as the habitable zone.

Earth's oceans, from warm tropical waters like these to freezing waters near the poles, are teeming with life.

The atmosphere spreads water over the Earth's surface, allowing animals and plants to live on land far from the oceans. Water evaporates from the oceans and moves with the winds.

It condenses to form clouds, and falls onto the surface as rain. This is part of circulation of water between the oceans, atmosphere and land, known as the water cycle.

Scientists think that most of the water on Earth came from volcanoes that erupted soon after the Earth was formed. Some of the water may have come from comets that collided with the Earth.

How life started

An amazing range of life survives on the Earth, from microscopic plankton in the sea to giant trees on the land. But there was no life when the Earth was formed about 4,600 million years ago. The surface was made of molten rock and there was no water or atmosphere. Hundreds of millions of years later the surface had cooled, but there were still many volcanoes erupting. These brought a mixture of chemicals to the surface. They mixed with pools of water, forming a chemical soup. The chemicals reacted together to form the complex chemicals that are the building blocks of all living things. Eventually, these chemicals came together to make the first, very simple forms of life.

Forms of life, such as these penguins, for example, survive in the most inhospitable regions of the world, from hot, dry deserts to the freezing poles.

27

Earth's Moon

The Moon is the Earth's only moon. It is about a quarter of the width of the Earth, making it one of the largest moons in the Solar System. Although the Moon is Earth's partner in space, it is a very different place. It is a dry, lifeless world, covered with craters. It looks the same now as it did thousands of millions of years ago.

Orbit and spin

The Moon completes its orbit of the Earth once every 27.3 days. The Moon also spins on its axis just as the Earth does, but very slowly. It completes one spin every time it orbits the Earth. This means that the same side of the Moon faces the Earth all the time. This side is known as the near side. The other side is known as the far side. The far side is always hidden from the Earth.

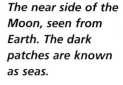

The near side of the Moon, seen from Earth. The dark patches are known as seas.

Much of our knowledge of the Moon comes from experiments carried out during the Apollo missions.

Craters and seas

The Moon's surface is smothered in craters. Some are a few metres across; others are hundreds of kilometres across. Most craters were formed by meteorites smashing into the Moon in its early life, more than 3,500 million years ago. The craters still exist because there is no erosion on the Moon. The large dark areas on the Moon are known as seas, but they don't contain water. They are giant impact craters that filled with lava that leaked from under the Moon's crust.

Phases and eclipses

The Sun lights up one side of the Moon. As the Moon orbits the Earth, it seems to change shape because we see different amounts of the lit side. A Full Moon is when we see the whole lit side. A New Moon is when we see none of it.

Sometimes the Earth, Moon and Sun are in a perfect straight line. This causes eclipses. A solar eclipse happens when the Moon is directly between the Earth and the Sun. The Moon's shadow falls on the Earth. Anybody in the shadow sees the Sun blocked out by the Moon. A lunar eclipse happens when the Earth is directly between the Sun and Moon. The Earth's shadow falls on the Moon, making it dark.

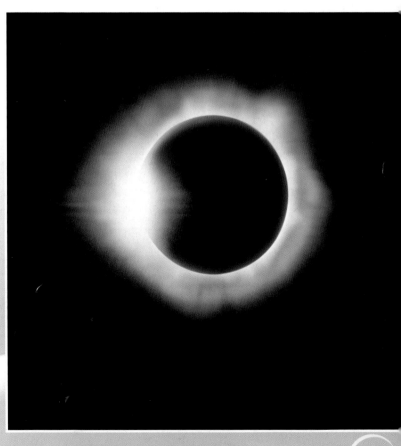

SPACE DATA

The Moon

Diameter:	3,476 km
Average distance from Earth:	384,400 km
Time to complete one spin:	27.3 Earth days
Lunar month:	29.5 Earth days
Gravity at surface:	0.17 x Earth gravity
Surface temperature:	-155°C to 105°C

During a total solar eclipse, gases are visible streaming from the Sun.

Mars

Mars is the fourth planet from the Sun. Although Mars is only half the size of Earth, and its mass is just one tenth of the mass of Earth, in other ways it is similar to Earth. Mars is known as the 'red planet' because its surface is covered with red-brown rock and dust.

Orbit and spin

Mars is the only rocky planet further from the Sun than the Earth. It takes nearly twice as long as the Earth to complete its orbit. The orbit is quite squashed, so that Mars comes as close as 200 million kilometres to the Sun, and reaches as far as 250 million kilometres from the Sun.

You can clearly see four giant volcanoes on this image of Mars.

The distance between Earth and Mars changes as the planets orbit the Sun. This makes Mars look larger and smaller at different times. It looks largest when it is closest to the Sun in its orbit, and the Earth is on the same side of the Sun as Mars. Then Mars is only about 50 million kilometres away.

Mars spins on its axis at a similar speed to the Earth. It completes one spin every 24.6 Earth hours. Its axis is also tilted over like the Earth's.

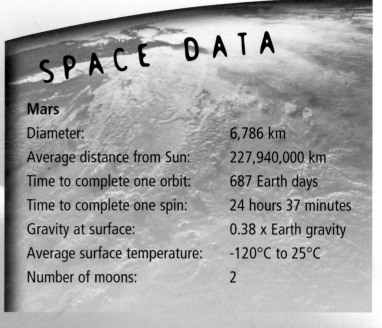

SPACE DATA

Mars

Diameter:	6,786 km
Average distance from Sun:	227,940,000 km
Time to complete one orbit:	687 Earth days
Time to complete one spin:	24 hours 37 minutes
Gravity at surface:	0.38 x Earth gravity
Average surface temperature:	-120°C to 25°C
Number of moons:	2

The atmosphere

Mars has a very thin atmosphere. It is two hundred times thinner than Earth's. More than 95 per cent of the atmosphere is carbon dioxide. The remainder is mainly nitrogen and argon. There is also some water vapour in the atmosphere, which sometimes forms thin clouds.

The Sun heats the surface of Mars, and the surface heats the gas in the atmosphere above. The heating effect is greater near the equator than at the poles, and this causes the gas to swirl about, creating winds. When Mars is at its closest to the Sun, the winds can reach 400 kilometres per hour. Even though the atmosphere is so thin, these strong winds can pick up dust from the surface, forming dust storms. These sometimes cover the whole surface, and take weeks to settle down again.

Internal structure

The internal structure of Mars is similar to the internal structure of the other rocky planets. It has three layers. They are a solid crust on the outside, a thick mantle, and a core. The upper mantle may be slightly molten, because some scientists think that volcanoes on Mars are still spewing out molten rock.

The core of Mars is probably solid. A liquid core would produce a magnetic field, and Mars does not have one.

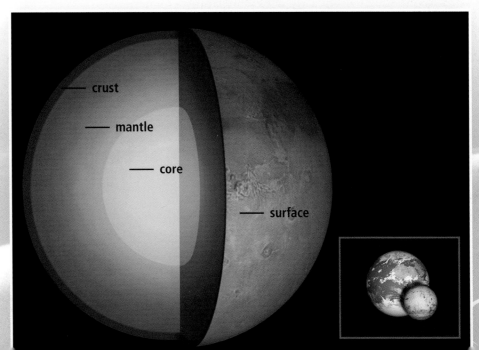

crust

mantle

core

surface

Mars: the Surface

The whole surface of Mars is covered with red-brown rocks and dust. There are several dramatic features, such as giant volcanoes and canyons, many times larger than the largest on Earth. The southern hemisphere has much older rocks than the northern hemisphere, and is much rougher, with many craters. The northern hemisphere is smoother, with fewer craters, but many volcanoes.

Giant volcanoes

Near the equator of Mars is an area where the surface bulges out. On top the bulge are three gigantic volcanoes. The largest of the three, called Olympus Mons, is the largest volcano in the whole Solar System. It is 26 kilometres high and 600 kilometres across at the base. These volcanoes are called shield volcanoes because they are very wide, with gentle slopes. They were formed by eruptions of runny lava over billions of years. So far, we haven't seen any of Mars's volcanoes erupting.

Looking straight down onto Olympus Mons. The crater in the middle is about 80 kilometres across.

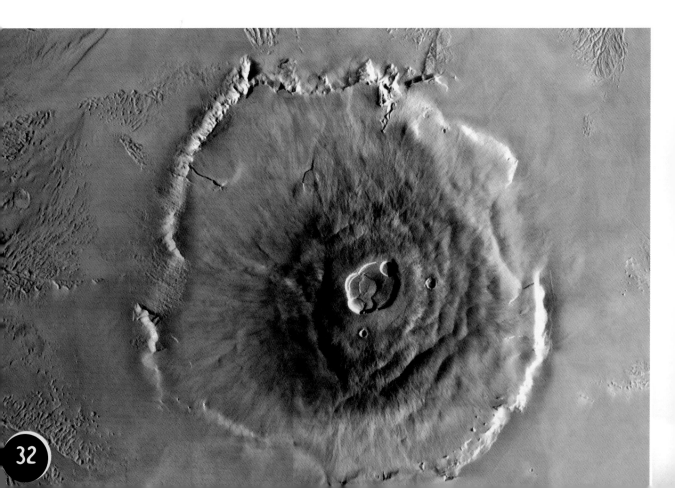

Canyons and valleys

Mars also features canyons and valleys. These are like dry rivers beds on Earth, and were probably formed by flowing water hundreds of millions of years ago. The largest canyon system is called the Valles Marineris. It stretches about 4,000 kilometres around the equator, and is up to 7 kilometres deep. It may be the remains of giant cracks that formed in the crust.

An impression of the view you would have from inside the giant Valles Marineris canyon on Mars.

Surface temperature

Because Mars is so far from the Sun, and because it has a very thin atmosphere that does not trap heat, its surface is very cold. On average, the temperature is −65°C.

Ice caps

Mars has ice caps at its poles. They are made up of a mixture of water ice (frozen water) and carbon dioxide ice. The ice caps grow in winter as the temperature falls, and water vapour and carbon dioxide from the atmosphere condense and turn solid. They shrink again in summer as the ice turns back to gas.

Space facts

Mars features

- The volcano Olympus Mons is three times taller than the Earth's tallest volcano, which forms the island of Hawaii.

- The channels on Mars were mistaken for canals by early astronomers. They thought the canals were built by a Martian civilisation.

Mars: Moons

Mars has two moons, called **Phobos and Deimos. They are tiny compared to most of the moons in the Solar System. The moons are so hard to spot from Earth that they were not discovered by astronomers until 1877. They are irregular in shape, rather than spherical, like Earth's Moon, and look like giant, dark potatoes.**

The moons of Mars, Phobos and Deimos, were discovered in 1877 by Asaph Hall, who named them after characters in Greek mythology.

Captured asteroids

Phobos and Deimos both appear to be asteroids. They were probably captured by the gravity of Mars as they drifted close to the planet. They may have come from the asteroid belt, between the orbits of Mars and Jupiter, where millions of asteroids orbit the Sun. Alternatively, the material that formed the moons may have been left over after the formation of Mars. Both moons orbit much closer to Mars than the Moon orbits Earth. And both spin round on themselves once per orbit, so that the same sides always face Mars.

Both moons are made of very dark rock. Both are also covered in craters, where they have been hit by other asteroids and meteorites. They are covered in a thin layer of dust created by the impacts. Gravity on the moons is extremely weak, but enough to keep the dust in place. Neither moon has an atmosphere.

Space Fact

● Phobos is a doomed moon. It is very gradually getting closer to Mars. In about 50 million years time, it will smash into the surface, creating a new crater.

Phobos, the larger moon of Mars. The dip on the left-hand end is a meteorite crater.

Phobos

Phobos is the larger moon, at 28 kilometres long. 'Phobos' is Greek for 'fear'. Phobos is between 18 and 22 kilometres across. At one end of Phobos is a huge crater, 10 kilometres across, which astronomers have named Stickney.

Phobos orbits Mars under 10,000 kilometres from the planet's centre. Because it is so close, it travels at very high speed. It completes a full orbit in just under 8 hours, which is only a third of a Mars day. Seen from Mars, Phobos moves quickly across the sky, in the opposite direction to the Sun and stars.

Deimos

Deimos is even smaller than Phobos, at just 16 kilometres long. It has a smoother, darker surface than Phobos, and fewer craters. It orbits further away from Mars, and more slowly than Phobos, taking about thirty hours to complete an orbit.

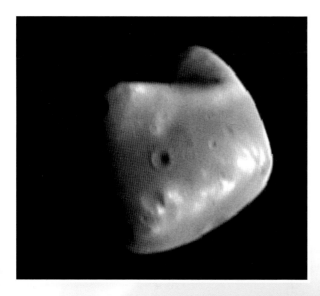

Deimos, the smaller moon of Mars. 'Deimos' is Greek for 'panic'.

Original and enhanced photographs of Phobos and Deimos taken by the Spirit *rover.*

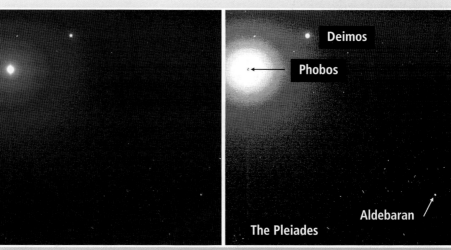

Deimos

Phobos

Aldebaran

The Pleiades

Mars: Water and Life

Astronomers think that if there is life anywhere else in the Solar System apart from Earth, then it is probably on Mars. So far we have found no trace of life, but that does not mean there isn't any. And life may have existed in the distant past.

Evidence for water

The forms of life we know on Earth can only exist where there is liquid water. There is water on Mars, but only in the form of gas in the atmosphere or ice on the surface. However, there may be liquid water under the surface. It could be in the form of ice in the soil. There may even be oceans of liquid water under the surface.

Ice and dust at the north pole of Mars. The ice is a mixture of frozen water and frozen carbon dioxide.

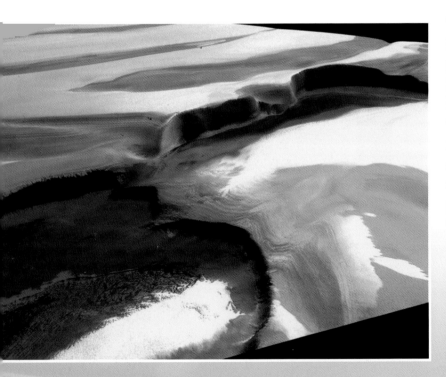

There was almost certainly liquid water on Mars in the past. The numerous channels in the surface could only have been formed by water flowing over thousands or millions of years. There are also flat areas alongside the channels that look like flood plains. Scientists are not sure where Mars's water came from, or where it went.

The search for life

It is impossible for life to exist on the surface of Mars today. There is no liquid water, it is extremely cold, the carbon dioxide in the atmosphere would be poisonous to animals, and the surface is bombarded with powerful and harmful rays from the Sun.

However, if there is liquid water under the surface, there may be life in the form of simple micro-organisms here. After all, simple forms of life survive in extreme places on Earth, such as near hot hydrothermal vents and at the poles.

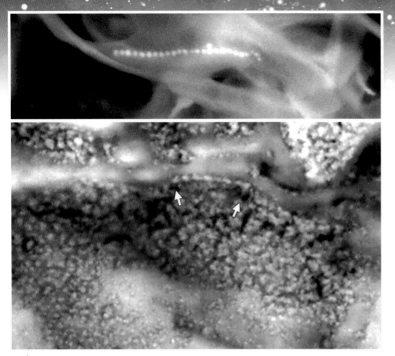

Scientists are not just looking for signs of life on Mars today, but for signs that it existed in the distant past.

Mars fossil

In 1984 a meteorite was found in Antarctica. Analysis of the rock it was made of showed that it could only have come from Mars. It was probably knocked off the planet by a meteorite impact. Inside the meteorite, known as ALH 84001, were tiny rounded lumps that looked like fossil bacteria. There was great excitement at the time, but today scientists think the lumps are tiny rock formations, and not fossils at all.

Top: bacteria from Earth. The bright chain is crystals in the bacteria. Bottom: a similar-looking chain in meteorite ALH 84001.

How do we know?

Mars rovers

Three robot vehicles have driven across the surface of Mars to take photographs and to analyse the rocks and soil. The first was *Sojourner*, in 1997, which was carried to the surface by the Mars *Pathfinder* probe. In 2004, two more rovers, *Spirit* and *Opportunity*, landed on opposite sides of the planet. *Opportunity* found evidence that the rocks had once been under water.

The rover Spirit *on the surface of Mars. Power for the motors and instruments comes from solar cells on top the body.*

How we Observe the Inner Planets

Our knowledge of the Earth and the other inner planets and their moons has come from making careful observations. We observe both from the Earth and from space. We also explore the other planets and moons by sending spacecraft to them. You can find out about exploration on page 40.

Telescopes

The main way of observing the planets (and moons) from Earth is by optical telescope. An optical telescope makes distant objects appear larger. There are two main types of telescope. A refracting telescope uses a lens to collect and focus the light. A reflecting telescope uses a mirror instead. The larger the mirror or lens, the more light that can be collected, and the more detail that can be seen in an object. Most astronomers use reflecting telescopes because they give clearer images. The image made by a telescope's lens or mirror is viewed with an eyepiece, or digitised so that it can be viewed and processed on a computer.

A clearer picture

The air in the Earth's atmosphere swirls about. This makes light from space bend slightly from side to side before it reaches the ground, which is why stars often twinkle at night. This makes it difficult for telescopes on the ground to get a clear picture of the planets. The largest research telescopes use a system called adaptive optics, which changes the shape of the mirror hundreds of times a second to cancel out the distortions caused by the atmosphere.

A hobby telescope like this gives good views of the Moon and planets.

Space telescopes

Space telescopes, such as the Hubble Space Telescope, are telescopes that are up in space. They have two advantages over ground-based telescopes. First, the atmosphere does not distort their images. Secondly, they can detect types of rays that cannot get through the Earth's atmosphere, such as X-rays and ultraviolet rays. Making images of these rays instead of light can tell us more about the planets.

The twin Keck telescopes on the island of Hawaii. Each telescope has a ten-metre wide main mirror.

Remote sensing

It is hard to observe the Earth from the Earth's surface. But we can get a good view from space, from remote-sensing satellites. From their orbits, these satellites can see a wide area of the Earth's surface. They carry a wide variety of sensors, to detect light and other forms of radiation, such as infra-red rays. Remote sensing is used to study the atmosphere, the oceans and the land.

Space Facts

Telescope tales

- Large research telescopes are normally situated on mountain tops to give a clearer view of the sky.

- The James Webb Space Telescope (see page 42) will have a 6.5-metre mirror. It will be able to see four hundred times the detail of a similar ground-based telescope.

How we Explore the Inner Planets

Although we can observe the other rocky planets from Earth with telescopes, they are so far away that we can't see much detail. To find out more, we send robot spacecraft called probes, which send back information for us.

Getting into space

Space is only a hundred kilometres away, but it is extremely hard to get there because of the Earth's gravity. A spacecraft must reach 28,000 kilometres per hour to stay in orbit, without falling back to Earth. Spacecraft need an enormous push to lift them into orbit and to reach orbital speed. They need extremely powerful launch vehicles, such as rockets and space shuttles. Their rocket engines produce huge thrust and also work in space, where there is no air. But once in orbit, no engines are needed because there is no air resistance.

An impression of the Phoenix *Mars Lander, which is due to be launched to Mars in 2007.*

Space Facts

- *Mariner 10* was the first probe to use a gravity assist. It used Venus's gravity to slow down so it could reach Mercury.

- Mars *Pathfinder* was the first probe to break its fall with airbags. Its designers got the idea from passenger air bags in cars.

Reaching other planets

Reaching the other planets is as difficult as getting into space in the first place. To escape Earth's gravity completely, and travel into the Solar System, a space probe must travel at about 40,000 kilometres per hour. Probes fly on a curved path (or trajectory) so that they meet a planet in its orbit. The path to the planet must be carefully planned, and the probe must be launched at a certain time if it is to intercept its target planet. The voyages take many months.

A probe often flies close to another planet on the way to its target planet. It uses the gravity of the planet to speed up, slow down or change direction. This is called a gravity assist, and it means the probe can carry much less fuel.

Orbiting and landing

Most probes go into orbit around another planet. Others are designed to land on the planet, or carry separate landers that they release to descend to the surface. Landers slow their descent with parachutes, or break their fall with air bags.

A Russian Soyuz-FG-Fregat launcher lifts off, carrying the Venus Express *probe into space.*

Anatomy of a probe

The main parts of a probe are its propulsion unit, a communications aerial, sensors that gather information, and a power source for its electronic circuits. The aerial detects radio signals from Earth that control the probe, and sends data signals back to Earth. Power comes from solar arrays or small nuclear power plants.

The Future

What is left to find out about the inner planets, and how will we observe them and explore them in the future? And what will happen to the inner planets, including the Earth, in the distant future?

In 2004, American President George W. Bush announced that a new manned space program would visit the Moon and Mars.

Future probes and observations

Several new space probe missions to the inner planets are planned. Probes will orbit the planets, mapping them in great detail, and probes will land to study their atmospheres, rocks, and to search for water and signs of life. New missions are also planned to find out more about the Moon.

More powerful telescopes, both on the ground and in space, will add to our knowledge of the planets. The replacement for the aging Hubble Space Telescope, called the James Webb Space Telescope, will give much clearer views of the planets after its launch which is scheduled for 2013.

Space Fact

- Following its launch, the James Webb Space Telescope will be sent into orbit 1.5 million km from the Earth. It will have a mirror measuring 6.5 m across and have a sunshield as big as a tennis court.

Man to Mars

The American space agency NASA is developing the successor to the space shuttle, called the Crew Exploration Vehicle. This will be launched by rocket. They plan to send astronauts to the Moon by 2020. They will explore the Moon, but also use the missions to test the technology for a manned mission to Mars. But years of work are needed to make sure their journey will be a safe one.

Perhaps we should try to reduce carbon emissions before spending fortunes on exploring the Solar System.

Earth's problems

Many scientists say that we should be solving problems on Earth before spending our resources to explore the other planets. The greatest issue is that of global warming and climate change, which need to be halted and reversed before they cause major problems for us. Other scientists argue that exploring will provide us with knowledge about how our own world works, and how it could change in the future.

Long term changes

Over millions of years, the Earth's surface will continue to change, with new mountain ranges forming and being eroded away again, and the continents drifting across the surface. Perhaps in the distant future it will look like Mars does today. The surfaces of Venus and Mars will change, too, as volcanoes continue to erupt. But Mercury will stay as it is today, a dead, unchanging world.

In about 5,000 million years time the Sun will run out of fuel. Then it will grow into a red ball of hot gas, so large that it will swallow up all the inner planets. They will all be destroyed.

Timeline of Discovery

1609   Astronomer Thomas Harriot uses a telescope to draw the first accurate map of the Moon.

1666   Giovanni Cassini discovers the Martian ice caps.

1877   Asaph Hall discovers the moons of Mars.

1959   *Luna 1* is the first probe to fly past the Moon.

1959   *Luna 3* is the first probe to see the far side of the Moon.

1962   *Mariner 2* is the first probe to fly past Venus.

1964   The first *Nimbus* remote-sensing satellite is launched for studying the oceans and atmosphere.

1965   *Mariner 4* is the first probe to photograph Mars after being launched the previous year.

1966   *Luna 9* is the first probe to make a successful landing on the Moon.

1969   Astronauts land on the Moon for the first time aboard *Apollo 11*.

1970   The first lunar rover, *Lunokhod 1*, lands on the Moon.

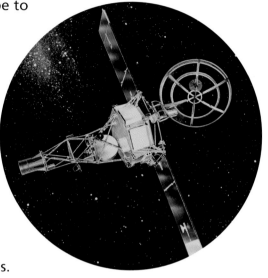

The probe Mariner 2, *the first probe to visit* Venus.

1970 *Venera 7* reaches the surface of Venus, the first probe to survive on the surface and send data back to Earth.

1972 The first Landsat satellite, *ERTS 1*, is launched to photograph and study the Earth's surface.

1974 *Mariner 10* flies past Mercury, taking photographs of the planet.

1975 *Venera 9* sends back the first photographs of the surface of Venus.

1989 The *Magellan* probe is launched and the following year maps the surface of Venus using radar.

1996 Mars *Global Surveyor* is launched. In 1997 it enters Mars's orbit and maps the surface of the planet.

1997 Mars *Pathfinder* lands on Mars after its launch the previous year. It carries a robot vehicle, called *Sojourner*, that drives slowly across the surface.

1998 *Lunar Prospector* orbits the Moon, and finds evidence of water ice in craters.

2006 *Venus Express* arrives in orbit around Venus.

The view of Mars from the Pathfinder *probe. The* Sojourner *rover is investigating the large, central rock.*

Glossary

asteroid A rocky object that orbits the Sun, but that is not large enough to be a planet. Most asteroids orbit between the orbits of Mars and Jupiter.

astronomer A scientist who studies planets, moons and other objects in space.

atmosphere A layer of gas that surrounds a planet or moon.

atmospheric pressure The push from the air on objects in the atmosphere.

comet A small, icy object that orbits the Sun.

condense To turn from gas to liquid.

continent A large land mass on the Earth (there are currently seven continents).

crater A dish-shaped hole in the surface of a planet or moon, created by an object from space smashing into the surface.

crust The solid, outer layer of the Earth.

erosion The gradual wearing away of the landscape by the weather and flowing water.

evaporate To turn from liquid to gas.

glacier A river of ice that flows slowly down from an ice-covered mountain range.

gravity A force that attracts all objects to each other.

hydrothermal vent A place on the ocean floor where hot water emerges from rocks underneath.

lava The name for molten rock after it comes from a volcano.

lunar To do with the Moon.

meteorite A rocky particle from space that crashes into the surface of a planet or moon.

moon An object that orbits around a planet, but that is not part of a planet's rings.

nebula A giant cloud of gas and dust in space.

nuclear reaction When the nucleus of an atom splits apart, or loses or gains some particles.

orbit 1) Moving around the Sun or a planet; 2) The path that an object takes as it moves around the Sun or a planet.

ozone A gas that is a special form of oxygen (each particle is made up of three oxygen atoms instead of the normal two).

planet An object in space that orbits around the Sun, but that is not part of a large group of objects, such as asteroids or comets.

probe A spacecraft sent into space to send back information about the Sun, other planets or moons.

satellite A spacecraft that orbits around the Earth.

solar array A panel of solar cells that turn sunlight into electricity.

tectonic plate One of the giant pieces that the Earth's crust is broken into.

water vapour The gas form of water, made when liquid water boils.

Further Information

Books

The Planets
David McNab and James Younger
BBC Worldwide, 1999

National Geographic Encyclopedia of Space
Linda K. Glover
National Geographic Society, 2005

Organizations

National Aeronautics & Space
Administration (NASA)
Organization that runs the US
space program
www.nasa.gov

International Astronomical Union (IAU)
The official world astronomy organization,
responsible for naming star, planets, moons
and other objects in space
www.iau.org

Jet Propulsion Laboratory (JPL)
Centre responsible for NASA's robot
space probes
www.jpl.nasa.gov

European Space Agency (ESA)
Organization responsible for space flight
and exploration of European countries
www.esa.int

The Planetary Society
Organization devoted to the exploration of
the Solar System
www.planetary.org

Websites

http://nssdc.gsfc.nasa.gov/planetary/
factsheet/
All the facts and figures you could ever
need about the inner planets

www.nineplanets.org
Lots of information about the planets

http://sse.jpl.nasa.gov/kids/index.cfm
NASA pages for children about exploring
the Solar System

http://dsc.discovery.com/guides/planetearth/
planetearth.html
Discovery Channel site about the Earth,
with interesting videos

http://mars.jpl.nasa.gov/funzone_flash.html
Fun activities all to with Mars

http://www.keckobservatory.org/
All about the Keck telescopes in Hawaii

Index

Numbers in **bold** indicate pictures.

THE EARTH AND SPACE

Contents of titles in the series:

WAYLAND